GEORGIAN DUBLIN

ARMS of the   of DUBLIN

JAMES MALTON

Georgian Dublin

TWENTY-FIVE AQUATINT VIEWS IN COLOUR
With an Introduction and Descriptive Notes by
MAURICE CRAIG

THE DOLMEN PRESS

James Malton's *Georgian Dublin*, reproduced in colour from the original aquatints etched for *A Picturesque and Descriptive View of the City of Dublin,* issued in monochrome in 1799 and later issued in colour aquatint, with an introduction by Maurice Craig, is printed in the Republic of Ireland for the publishers, THE DOLMEN PRESS, Mountrath, Portlaoise, Ireland. The book is designed by Liam Miller and printed by Irish Printers Limited. The plates are reproduced from copies in the National Library of Ireland by kind permission of the Director and Trustees; the colour photography is by Eugene Hogan.

First published 1984

British Library Cataloguing in Publication Data
Malton, James
Georgian Dublin.
1. Malton, James   2. Dublin (Dublin) in art
I. Title
769.92'4   NE2047.6.M/

ISBN 0 85105 424 2
ISBN 0 85105 425 0 *paperback*

CONTENTS

Introduction *by* Maurice Craig   *page* vii

PLATES
from
A PICTURESQUE AND DESCRIPTIVE VIEW
OF THE CITY OF DUBLIN

Engraved Title.
Arms of Dublin.
Engraved Dedication.

The twenty-five aquatint Views follow in the order printed in Malton's prospectus. The titles given here are those on the engravings. Plate 25a is a monochrome key to the Views in Plates 24 and 25.

1   Great Court Yard, Dublin Castle.
2   The Parliament House, Dublin.
3   Trinity College, Dublin.
4   College Library, Dublin.
5   Provost's House, Dublin.
6   Saint Patrick's Cathedral, Dublin.
7   West Front of St. Patrick's Cathedral.

8   Royal Exchange, Dublin.
9   Custom House, Dublin.
10   View of the Law-Courts, looking up the Liffey, Dublin.
11   Tholsel, Dublin.
12   Old Soldiers Hospital, Kilmainham, Dublin.
13   Royal Infirmary, Phoenix Park, Dublin.
14   Blue-Coat Hospital, Dublin.
15   Lying-in Hospital, Dublin.
16   Rotunda & New Rooms, Dublin.
17   St. Catherine's Church, Thomas Street, Dublin.
18   Marine School, Dublin, looking up the Liffey.
19   Leinster House, Dublin.
20   Charlemont-House, Dublin.
21   Powerscourt-House, Dublin.
22   View from Capel Street, looking over Essex Bridge, Dublin.
23   St. Stephen's Green, Dublin.
24   Barracks, Dublin.
25   View of Dublin, from the Magazine, Phoenix-Park.
25a   (Key Plate to the Barracks, and distant View of Dublin.)

MALTON'S *Dublin* has been called 'one of the most beautiful books of the art of aquatint.' Though it is only the third illustrated book on Dublin ever to appear (its predecessors being Walter Harris's *History* of 1766 and Pool and Cash's *Views* of 1780) it is by far the most splendid, and it is extremely unlikely that anything comparable will ever again be done. Its author James Malton, who for all the evidence to the contrary seems to have written the text as well as doing the drawings and engraving them, came of a family notable in the sphere of topographical and architectural draughtsmanship. His father Thomas, born in 1726, wrote text books on geometry and perspective drawing and seems to have spent the last fifteen years of his life in Dublin, where it is said he lived by lecturing on those subjects. Thomas had two sons, Thomas the younger born in 1748, and James, the date of whose birth is not known. The three Maltons are very confusing and have confused many people. All three died at much the same time: Thomas the elder in 1801, Thomas the younger in 1804, and James in 1803. To confuse matters still further, it was not James, the 'Dublin' Malton, who died in Dublin, but his father. One at least of the Maltons, probably our James, almost certainly spent some time in James Gandon's office during the building of the Custom House, probably from 1781 to 1784. If he was then 'a youth of seventeen' he would have been born in about 1764 and will have done his great Dublin series when in his late twenties and early thirties. It is, however, just possible that one of the Maltons was articled to Gandon in London in about 1767, and if so James would have been born in about 1750 which fits his brother's age better. The assertions here repeated come from the *Life of Gandon* of 1846 and from an anonymous book called *Letters to Parliament* which appeared in Dublin in 1787 and may be by one of the Maltons. Their testimony is contradictory and unclear, but it seems that there were two points at which Gandon and the Maltons crossed each other's paths: in or about 1769 when Gandon came second in the Royal Exchange Competition, and in or about 1781 and following years. On both occasions one of the Maltons is alleged to have attacked Gandon in print. But no pamphlet of about 1769 fitting the required description has so far come to light. The 1787 book, however, is virulently anti-Gandon.

Both the Gandon-Malton episodes, it will be noticed, take place against a Dublin background. But this gives the impression that James Malton's contact with Dublin was of much longer duration than in fact it was. Neither he nor his father appear in the Dublin directories, and James himself tells us in his Preface that 'the entire of the views were taken in 1791, by the Author', and through he claims to have kept all the subjects under observation till 1797 so that they would all be correctly represented as they actually were, the plates are all dated from London by James Malton, except for those (a majority: fourteen out of twenty-five) where the name of Malton in London is joined with that of George Cowen in Dublin. It seems overwhelmingly probable that

after his year or so of activity here he returned to London with his drawings, notes and other material to work them up for publication. The latest date — that on the plate of the Four Courts — is 1799.

The author of the *Life of Gandon* asserts that Malton's letter-press descriptions of Gandon's buildings were 'envenomed with the most malignant misrepresentations', but no trace of this is to be found in any of the editions which I have seen. On the contrary, the descriptions of the Custom House and Four Courts are appreciative, unless perhaps we are to suspect that his tone is ironical when he writes, of the central hall of the Four Courts, that it is 'so extremely beautiful that no verbal description can convey an adequate idea of it; 'tis simple! 'tis elegant! 'tis magnificent!' Of Gandon's other Dublin buildings, the King's Inns is too late in date for Malton's attention, and while Malton did draw a view of College Green looking through the new portico of the House of Lords on what was shortly to become Westmoreland Street, it is perhaps significant that he did not engrave it.

The discrepancies between Malton's prints of the Custom House and Four Courts and the executed buildings (particularly glaring in the case of the Four Courts, for which see my notes opposite the plate) seem to me a clear indication that Malton was still, by 1799, on such bad terms with Gandon that he could not do as artists normally did with unfinished buildings: procure drawings from the architect and work from them. In every other instance he was extremely accurate.

Not only was Malton consummately skilful at drawing architecture; his ability to people the streets with realistic life and to convey an atmosphere of arcadian clarity makes up a large part of his appeal. No doubt, as the Knight of Glin suggests, the streets were not quite so clean as he shows them, nor the painted carriages always so sparklingly fresh. And it is we, rather than Malton, who bring to our view of these elegant scenes the hindsight of the long anti-climax of the nineteenth century.

It is the coloured version, such as we have here, which elicits these reflexions. The best authorities seem to be agreed that the original issues of the plates were all uncoloured, and one goes so far as to say that it is 'doubtful if copies were issued in colour until a period approaching 1820.' There seems to be general agreement that copies intended to be coloured were inked in a lighter tone than those intended to remain uncoloured. Needless to say the higher price obtainable for the coloured versions has caused a great many to be coloured more or less skilfully by later hands, but the detection of these is largely a matter of connoisseurship, experience and flair.

The essence of the aquatint process is the laying down on the plate of a minutely granulated layer of asphaltum or rosin so that the acid pits the plate to a very fine grain which catches the ink in such a way that it prints like a watercolour wash. It seems that the plate could be printed at first in two colours or perhaps three, black or grey and perhaps a blue for the sky, and afterwards further coloured by hand in the engraver's studio before being issued. The process, though invented a century earlier in Holland, was brought to England by Gandon's great friend

Paul Sandby, and a letter from Sandby to Gandon in 1783 mentions 'young Malton' who is, most probably, our James. But of course if the coloured Maltons were not issued until after James's death in 1803 he is unlikely to have coloured them or supervised their colouring. Very oddly, as it seems to us, the same price was originally charged for both the coloured and uncoloured versions: ten guineas the set.

For a good many of the subjects there exist original Malton water-colour drawings which do give authority for the best of the coloured sets, such as that used for this modern reprint. Most of these watercolours are in the National Gallery of Ireland and some in Trinity College Dublin, the British Museum and the Victoria and Albert Museum in London. There are two also at Mount Stewart, Co. Down, and two in the Huntington Library, California.

James's brother Thomas Malton drew similar subjects in a similar style but was more prolific. His London and Westminster series of 100 prints, issued between 1792 and 1801, and his Oxford series of 24 issued between 1802 and 1803, as well as his Bath views, are naturally very popular in England, but have never been quite so highly esteemed as the Dublin set. Thomas Malton did draw one Irish subject, the interior of the Assembly Rooms, Belfast, which had been created by Sir Robert Taylor inside the old Exchange there in 1776, and formed part of a series of 32 Malton aquatints of Taylor's works. Doubtless it was done from Taylor's drawings.

The elder Malton also drew one Irish subject, the interior of Christ Church (Church of Ireland) Cathedral, Waterford, which was engraved by John Roberts the Cathedral's architect, perhaps in about 1780. It should be added also that the pair of interior perspectives, of Waterford Courthouse and Coolbanagher Church, of which one is in the National Gallery of Ireland and the other in the church itself, which I believe to be probably by James Gandon, are believed by others to be by one of the Maltons.

In my young days every doctor and dentist in or near Fitzwilliam Square had a set of Malton's Dublin hanging in his waiting-room or on the stairs. They have now become much too rare and valuable to be used in this way, but the present volume gives them a fresh lease of life on a less exalted plane. James Malton was as fortunate in Dublin as Dublin was in him. There is no reason to doubt the sincerity of his protestation in his prospectus, that 'views of profit have been but a secondary consideration in the conduct of this work: Mr. Malton was struck with admiration at the beauty of the capital of Ireland, and was desirous to make a display of it to the World.' And so he did, and does, and in his two dozen blinks of the shutter makes time, for a moment, stand still.

TO THE

Right Honorable the Lord Mayor,

ALDERMEN, SHERIFFS, COMMON-COUNCIL, FREEMEN, AND

Citizens OF THE CITY OF Dublin.

This Work,

Intended to contain a concise yet complete Description of the

CAPITAL OF IRELAND:

Is humbly Dedicated and given to Their Protection by Their

Obedient Humble Servant

James Malton.

London June 1.st 1794

A

Picturesque AND Descriptive

View of the City of

DUBLIN

DISPLAYED

In a Series of the most Interesting Scenes taken in the Year 1791

By James Malton

With

A brief authentic History from the earliest accounts to the

Present Time

I

The building on the right, which recently housed the Genealogical Office and was the scene of the theft of the 'Irish Crown Jewels' in 1907, is of the early eighteenth century and very probably by Sir Edward Lovett Pearce. It resembles Lord Pembroke's Villa in Whitehall, London, by Roger Morris, though in Malton's day the attic storey, which greatly increased the resemblance, had not yet been added. Visible above the West range is the tower and spire of St. Werburgh's Church, which were taken down in 1810 and 1836, ostensibly because they were unsafe but more probably for the security of the Castle. The portico of the State Apartments seen on the left of the picture is, like the rest of the buildings (except for the attic storey) unchanged today.

GREAT COURT YARD, DUBLIN CASTLE.

2

THE PARLIAMENT HOUSE

This is the plate which in an early state had three pigs in the foreground, being driven by the man on the left with outstretched stick. Only his dog survived the purge. Malton has chosen his viewpoint and direction to show only Pearce's 1729 South colonnade and not the curved additions to East and West, by Gandon and Park respectively, which at this time (1793) differed from each other. The windows behind the columns still light rooms in the Parliament House, which still had seven years to go. The West Front of Trinity College, of 1752–9, has not changed, and only the distant houses on the North side of College Street have been replaced. The spectator of 1793 would have seen the equestrian statue of King William III, just out of frame to the left.

THE PARLIAMENT HOUSE — DUBLIN

3

TRINITY COLLEGE

Credit for this design was until recently given to Keene and Saunderson of London (Henry Keene 1726–76 and John Saunderson who died in 1774) but Dr Edward McParland has recently *established that the architect was Theodore Jacobsen who had already designed the Foundling Hospital in London. The Irish Parliament made generous grants for this West front and the whole of Parliament Square, and it was built between 1752 and 1759, of Irish granite with Portland stone dressings. The low railings seen in this plate have since been replaced by loftier railings by Richard Turner, the Dublin ironfounder.

Country Life, 13 May, 1976, pp. 1244-5.

TRINITY COLLEGE, DUBLIN.

4

This view of the interior of Thomas Burgh's great Library of 1712–32 shows it before the alterations of 1857, when the flat plaster ceiling was replaced by Benjamin Woodward with a semicircular barrel-vault of timber. Trinity Library remains one of the largest single-chamber libraries in existence, comparable to the much later Bibliothèque Sainte Geneviève beside the Panthéon in Paris. The ground-floor arcade was originally intended to insulate the books from the damp of the low marshy ground on which, like Wren's Library at Trinity College Cambridge, it was built. But in the 1890's the arcade was glazed in and the space devoted to book-storage. Originally a wall divided the South-facing cloister towards the Fellows' Garden from the North-facing cloister towards Library Square.

COLLEGE LIBRARY, *DUBLIN.*

5

PROVOST'S HOUSE

Here, too, Dr McParland has cast convincing doubt on the traditional attribution.* The Provost's House, begun in 1769 by Provost Andrews, may well have been supervised by John Smyth the architect of St Catherine's and St Thomas's churches. But it is more than likely that above and behind him was Henry Keene. The front facade, however, was taken from Lord Burlington's house for General Wade in what is now Old Burlington Street, London, which, in turn, was taken from a drawing by Palladio in Lord Burlington's collection. The internal arrangements, however, are indebted neither to Palladio nor to Burlington, and are of the utmost splendour. The house is now the only large eighteenth-century town house in Dublin still occupied as a private residence. Rising over the buildings of Library Square may be seen the dome of the then Chapel. By 1791 the tower and dome (more or less half-way between the present Chapel and Examination Hall) had become unsafe, and were shortly taken down. The gates of the Provost's House are still there but the wall is now surmounted by railings.

PROVOST'S HOUSE, DUBLIN.

6

SAINT PATRICK'S CATHEDRAL

This view is particularly valuable because it shows the Cathedral before any of the nineteenth-century restorations which began with Carpenter's rebuilding of the Lady Chapel (on the right) in the 1840's, and continued under Sir Benjamin Guinness some twenty years later. The panelled pinnacles so clearly visible here above the flying buttresses of the choir can be traced at least as far back as the plate in Ware's *Antiquities* of 1739. The greatest visible changes have taken place at the West end of the South side, where an eighteenth-century building can be seen half-hidden by the transept-end. But on the whole it is remarkable how little this scene, though less spacious today, has changed.

SAINT PATRICK'S CATHEDRAL, DUBLIN.

7

WEST FRONT OF ST PATRICK'S CATHEDRAL

Even in 1793 St Patrick's was visibly sited in a depression, as this plate shows. The great West window was re-mediaevalised in the Victorian restorations. Early in the present century the Iveagh Trust swept away the whole area of poor streets between the Cathedral and Christ Church Place — Bull Alley, Bride Alley, Ross Lane and the rest — including many houses of the 'Dutch Billy' type such as can be seen on the left of this plate, which were once common not only in Dublin but in many provincial towns. Cross Poddle is reputed to be the shortest street in Dublin. It is now called Dean Street.

WEST FRONT of S.ᵗ PATRICK'S CATHEDRAL

8

ROYAL EXCHANGE

The famous Wide Streets Commissioners were first brought into being in 1757 to make a convenient street from Capel Street Bridge to Dublin Castle. Their operations produced a hundred-foot square site dominating the approach to the bridge, and here it was resolved to build an Exchange. A competition was held in 1769, and 61 designs were sent in, 25 of which were from Ireland and 33 from England. Thomas Cooley was the winner, followed by James Gandon, second, and Thomas Sandby, third, all of London. Consisting originally of one basic space, within which the ring of columns rose to support the dome, the Royal Exchange, with its fastidious detailing, set a new standard for Dublin and heralded the era of neo-classicism. It passed through various vicissitudes before becoming the City Hall in 1852 and suffering encroachment on its unified space by having office-rooms carved out of it. It remains, nevertheless, one of the finest eighteenth-century interiors in the city.

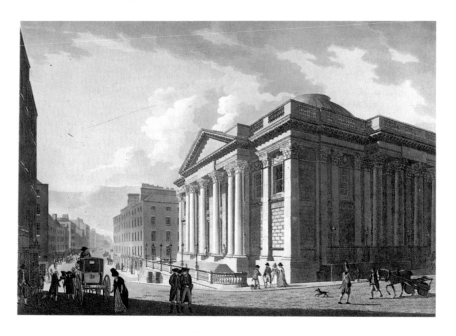

ROYAL EXCHANGE, DUBLIN.

9

The Custom House, perhaps the most famous building in Dublin, was begun in 1781 from the designs of James Gandon, and must have been virtually completed by the time (1792) of this plate. It is known, however, that James Malton, who had been employed by Gandon during the early years of its construction, was by then on bad terms with him. The usual procedure for topographical artists depicting buildings in progress was to get drawings and information from the architect. This perhaps explains why, in this otherwise very accurate plate — understandably one of the most popular of the series — the 'soup-tureen' urns on the corner-pavilions (over the window one bay back from the river-front) are omitted. Other respects in which this representation differs from what is to be seen now are the niches alternating with windows on the first floor over the arcades, the four statues, now absent from their positions over the main portico, and the roof of the Long Room just visible here behind the dome. All these differences are the result of the alterations made when the building was restored by the Board of Works after its gutting by fire in 1921.

CUSTOM HOUSE, DUBLIN.

THE LAW COURTS (FOUR COURTS)

This must have been one of the last of the plates to be completed, because the Four Courts was still not finished at the time of the Union of 1800 and this plate is dated 1799, notwithstanding that Malton says in his preface that ' the work was in hand till 1797'. It is among the least satisfactory of the series, for reasons mostly connected with the bad feeling between Malton and Gandon (already mentioned in connection with the Custom House plate). The insertion of round-headed windows instead of square-headed in the ground floor fronts of the wings is perhaps a trivial discrepancy. Much more serious is Malton's failure to give any adequate impression of the dominating grandeur of the dome, which is, also, depicted as less shallow than it was in reality. (In the reconstruction after 1922 its very subtle outline was not quite faithfully reproduced). The dies over the central windows of the wings, ignorantly omitted in the trimmed-back reconstruction, were replaced by the Board of Works under the late Gerald McNicoll in the early 1970's. Malton's view was taken from Ormonde Bridge which stood opposite Ormonde Market and was swept away in a flood in 1802. Its successor Richmond Bridge (O'Donovan Rossa) was built further upstream in 1813–16. In the distance is Dublin Bridge or the Old Bridge, the only bridge for many centuries, rebuilt in 1816–17 as Whitworth Bridge and in our time renamed after Father Theobald Mathew. The houses on the left remind us that the South Quays were not finally cleared of obstructions until the early nineteenth century.

VIEW OF THE LAW-COURTS, LOOKING UP THE LIFFEY, DUBLIN.

11

THE THOLSEL

This building has been among the missing for longer than any other subject in the Malton series. It was built, as the then equivalent of the City Hall, in 1676, to a pattern familiar from the middle ages onwards in many English towns: an open arcade surmounted by accommodation such as council-room, court-room and rudimentary offices. The master-builder Thomas Graves constructed it and may well have designed it as well. As drawn by the visitor Thomas Dineley in 1680, it agreed very closely with what is to be seen in this plate, with the addition of a steeple-like structure on top, with an arcade, a clock-face and finally a little pudding-bowl cupola. This no doubt disappeared fairly early on, as such structures generally do unless carefully maintained. But the Tholsel itself lasted until about 1806 when is had become so unsafe that it had to be taken down. It was typical merchants' architecture, and had it survived till now would be thought very picturesque. It stood to the South of Christ Church Cathedral, in Skinners' Row, later widened as Christ Church Place.

THOLSEL, *DUBLIN.*

THE ROYAL HOSPITAL KILMAINHAM

Begun in 1679 to the designs of Sir William Robinson the Surveyor-General of Ireland, Kilmainham Hospital was a home for old soldiers modelled on Les Invalides in Paris, and such as was, slightly later, built at Chelsea by Sir Christopher Wren. The building surrounds a nearly square courtyard, with arcaded walks over which are corridors giving access to the 'wards'. The North-West corner (to the right in the plate) contained the quarters of the Commander-in-Chief who was ex-officio Master of the hospital. The three bays of the projection on which stands the tower, and one bay on each side of it, correspond to the Great Hall which is 98 feet by 46 feet. Beyond it to the East is the Chapel, of which two and a half windows may here be seen. The tower and spire, though intended from the beginning, were not added until shortly after 1700. It is noteworthy that whereas the windows of the Master's quarters (which extend upwards through two floors) have 'Georgian' glazing, those of the tower and chapel have Y-mullions and otherwise resemble those of, for example, St Mary's Church in Mary Street. This print proves that this kind of fenestration, even if it looks Victorian, is sometimes original and older. At the end of the terrace the house of the Deputy Adjutant-General is early eighteenth-century but was adroitly enlarged some time in the nineteenth. The whole building is at the time of writing being rehabilitated to serve as a conference-centre, with public access to the more noteworthy parts. After the dissolution of the Hospital in 1927 the building served for about twenty years as the administrative headquarters of the Garda Síochána, but has since been empty except for use as storage. When it is again open the people of Ireland will again be able to enjoy one of their most splendid possessions.

OLD SOLDIERS HOSPITAL, KILMAINHAM, DUBLIN.

13

ROYAL MILITARY INFIRMARY

Apart from the vanished Tholsel, this must be the least-known of the buildings here illustrated, though it has stood in almost unaltered form in the Phoenix Park for nearly two hundred years. It was designed by Gandon — a circumstance which Malton omits to mention — but carried out by the Board of Works architect William Gibson, and opened in 1788. It is not one of Gandon's most distinguished designs, and has not been improved by the alteration of the central openings some time during the nineteenth century. It is now Army Headquarters.

ROYAL INFIRMARY, PHOENIX PARK, DUBLIN.

BLUE-COAT HOSPITAL

The King's Hospital or Blue-Coat School had been settled in North-West Dublin since 1675, before its recent move to Palmerstown. Originally it stood on Oxmantown Green, a little to the West of Queen Street, but after an architectural competition won by Thomas Ivory it was rebuilt in 1773 somewhat further West. Ivory's elegant design, the subject of this plate, was not carried out in its entirety. The original very beautiful drawings now in the British Library, London, provided for buildings round a square court at the back, and neither these, nor the tall steeple over the central entrance shown here, were executed. But the uncompleted tower up to the lower of the two sets of round headed windows stood for many years until in 1894 it was taken down and replaced by the present cupola designed by R.J. Stirling. For a few years after the School moved out the building stood empty, but it has since been reconditioned and occupied by the Incorporated Law Society who formerly had accommodation in the Four Courts.

BLUE-COAT HOSPITAL DUBLIN.

15

LYING-IN HOSPITAL (THE 'ROTUNDA')

The Hospital, the first of its kind in Ireland or Great Britain, was promoted by the remarkable Dr Bartholomew Mosse, designed by Richard Castle or Cassels, begun in 1751 and opened in 1757. The main block bears a fairly close resemblance to Leinster House by the same architect: not surprisingly since both are in essence the application of a country-house type of design to a site which was then (in both cases) on the edge of the town. The Hospital is distinguished by its cupola (which unlike that of the King's Hospital School did get built). There was originally a gilded cradle, crown and ball, as a vane surmounting it; but this did not last long. The curved colonnaded wings terminated originally in smaller and simpler pavilions than those shown here, which are part of Gandon's work of 1784 and show his characteristic triumphal arch motif, inset columns, and urns. The pavilion on the left has been destroyed and its place taken by the hospital extension: that on the right is still there but almost invisible under sign-boards etc. The Rotunda proper, which has given the whole complex its name, is seen in the distance but from closer up in the next plate.

LYING-IN HOSPITAL, DUBLIN.

ROTUNDA NEW ROOMS

The Rotunda itself, designed by John Ensor and built in 1764, became the centrepiece of the constellation of pleasure-rooms which brought in an income to support the hospital. With an internal diameter of 80 feet, it was at first a rather dull brick building externally. But in 1784 many additions were made: the new Assembly Rooms planned by the amateur architect Michael Frederick Trench of Heywood, but with elevations by Richard Johnston, the heightening of the Rotunda wall by Gandon who enriched it with Coade stone ornaments by Edward Smyth, and the addition of the pavilions of which one is visible on the left of this plate. The Rotunda, after more than a century of miscellaneous use, is now a cinema, and since 1930 the Gate Theatre has occupied the Great Supper Room, adapted by Michael Scott. The Ballroom underneath was till lately in use as a dance-hall, but is now to be cut up and used as laboratories. The houses on the right, in Cavendish Row otherwise Rutland Square East otherwise Parnell Square East, date from the mid-1750's and are among the grandest in Dublin, with magnificent interiors some of which survive while others have fallen on evil days.

ROTUNDA & NEW ROOMS, DUBLIN.

17

ST CATHERINE'S CHURCH

Like several other churches in Dublin, St Catherine's never got the tower which it was intended to have, and still has its perfunctorily capped-off appearance as it had in 1797. The magnificently rugged doric granite front was conservatively repaired in 1975 by Dublin Corporation. The church itself ceased to be used some years ago, and after a period of some anxiety was acquired by a trust in 1970 and functions as an arts centre, concert-hall etc. More recently a monument commemorating Robert Emmet, who was hanged in front of the church in 1803, has been placed near the North-West door. The scene is very little changed since Malton's time: even the pub which now occupies the place of the blank-walled building in the right-centre of the picture is of about the same shape and size as its predecessor. The date of the church is 1769 and the architect was John Smyth who designed also St Thomas Malborough Street, (destroyed in 1922) and was concerned also with the Provost's House in Trinity College and with the Poolbeg lighthouse.

St CATHARINE'S CHURCH, THOMAS STREET, DUBLIN.

THE MARINE SCHOOL

This print is really a view of the approach to Dublin by sea, with the Custom House dome conspicuous in the distance on the right, rather than a view of the Hibernian Marine School which is on the left and much closer to the spectator. The school, which was for the sons of seamen and prepared the boys both for the merchant marine and for the Royal Navy, was started at Ringsend — a traditionally seafaring centre — in 1766, and moved to new buildings on Sir John Rogerson's Quay in 1773. The early authorities disagree about the authorship of the building: some give it to Thomas Cooley but Malton in his text gives it to Thomas Ivory. Cooley seems on the whole more probable. As may be seen, it was a plain but substantial building. The two wings, of which the West was the Chapel and the East (here visible) the School-room, were somewhat more elaborate. The school moved out in 1872, and the building became a cold storage depot. As such it survived though in mutilated and obscured form for a very long time, but was finally demolished in 1979 or 1980. Even now, however, the fronts of the wings still stand.

MARINE SCHOOL, DUBLIN. LOOKING UP THE LIFFEY.

19

LEINSTER HOUSE

The 20th Earl of Kildare's decision to build, in 1744, a palatial house on what was then called Molesworth Fields, at the edge of the town, gave a marked character to this quarter of Dublin, a character which it has never since quite lost. His architect Richard Cassels had, a year or two earlier, built a large detached house for the Earl of Tyrone in Marlborough Street on the North side of the river. But Kildare House was much larger, and by its axial placing it dominated Molesworth Street as it was later to dominate the large-scale development of Merrion Square, begun in 1762. In plan and character it is more a country house than a town one, and apart from redecorations of some rooms by Chambers in 1767 and Wyatt in 1794, it has survived with little alteration. The Duke of Leinster (as he had by then become) stayed on for fourteen years after the Union, but in 1814 Leinster House was sold to the (not yet 'Royal') Dublin Society, whose headquarters it remained for over a hundred years. In the years following 1877 the National Museum and National Library were built on the South and North sides of its forecourt; buildings of similar cultural purpose were already in place on its Eastern side. The latest change came when in 1924 the two houses of the Oireachtas, Dáil and Seanad, moved into Leinster House, an arrangement which is very far from ideal and becomes less and less appropriate as the years go by. Queen Victoria's statue has come and gone, and now, apart from the mutilation of the short colonnades to right and left, Leinster House looks much as it did in 1792, the date of Malton's plate.

LEINSTER HOUSE, DUBLIN.

20

CHARLEMONT HOUSE

Built in 1762 onwards by Sir William Chambers for the first Earl of Charlemont, Charlemont House took up a plot of triple width in the middle of the North side of Parnell Square, then called Palace Row, and stood detached from its neighbours. It was famous in the eighteenth century for its library and artistic contents and for the civilised life led by the Earl and his circle. It was sold to the government in 1870 and became the General Registry of Births, Marriages and Deaths. In 1929 it was handed over to the Dublin Corporation who demolished a great part of it, keeping only the front rooms, and altering the door-case. More recently the obelisks (visible in the print) have been reinstated. The small building in the foreground is one of a pair of shelters for the sedan-chair-men which were demolished in about 1943. The part of the former Rotunda Gardens immediately facing Charlemont House has been laid out as the Garden of Remembrance, designed by Daithi Hanly. Since 1931 Charlemont House has been the Municipal Gallery of Modern Art, now known as the Hugh Lane Gallery.

CHARLEMONT-HOUSE, DUBLIN.

21

POWERSCOURT HOUSE

Lord Powerscourt had already had his grand house in Co Wicklow for thirty years when in 1771 he employed Robert Mack to design this large house in a rather narrow street. The design was already somewhat old-fashioned by the time the house was built, in 1774. The right-hand wing archway led into the stable-yard behind while that on the left led to the kitchens. The tall attic over the pediment is said to have been used as an observatory. On the right appears part of the exhibition gallery built by the Society of Artists in 1765–71, which later became the City Assembly Room and was used among other things as a court-room. It is now the Municipal Museum and houses the collections assembled by the Old Dublin Society. The four houses beyond Powerscourt House are of similar date or a little earlier and have so far survived. At the time of writing an extensive scheme of remodelling is being carried out in the buildings at the rere of Powerscourt House, erected for the Stamp Office after 1807. From 1835 until recently the main house was occupied by Messrs Ferrier, Pollock, wholesale drapers, who looked after it very well.

POWERSCOURT-HOUSE, DUBLIN.

22

VIEW FROM CAPEL STREET

Parliament Street, the first work of the Wide Streets Commissioners, made in 1758, appears clearly in this print, leading to the Royal Exchange of 1769. Essex Bridge, by George Semple, succeeded Sir Humphrey Jervis's bridge which began to decay in 1751. Semple's bridge, of which he was justifiably proud, was opened in 1755. It was closely modelled on Westminster Bridge by Charles Labelye, but wider and of course shorter. It was built by the then novel method of coffer-dams which were kept pumped dry of water. It lasted till 1874 when it was replaced by the present Grattan Bridge. The building with the dormer windows beyond the ship's mast is the Old Custom House by Thomas Burgh, built in 1707 which remained in use till the new one was opened in 1791. The shop on the corner with the round-headed windows was till fairly recently Lemass the outfitters, and remained comparatively unchanged. There is perhaps more street-life to be seen in this print than in any other of Malton's.

VIEW FROM CAPEL-STREET, LOOKING OVER ESSEX-BRIDGE DUBLIN.

23

ST STEPHEN'S GREEN

This plate is taken from near the North-West corner of the Green, looking towards the Leeson Street corner. The Green had been a common since mediaeval times, but in 1662 it was emparked by the Corporation as a more or less regular rectangle and the lots on each side let out for building, the rents to go to the support of the King's Hospital School. Later the four sides came to be known as the Beaux' Walk (North), Leeson's Walk (South), Monk's Walk (East) and French Walk (West). The statue in the middle is of George II, by John Van Nost. It was later raised up on an earthen mound, but, as too often happens to Dublin statues, it was blown up about fifty years ago. To the right, and just to the left of the tree-trunk, may be seen Clanwilliam House No 85 St Stephen's Green, by Richard Cassels (1739) and its taller neighbour Buck Whaley's house No 86, by Robert West (1765) which together now constitute Newman House, named in honour of John Henry Cardinal Newman founder of the Catholic University, and now in the occupation of University College which has otherwise mostly migrated to Belfield.

S.ᵗ STEPHEN'S GREEN, DUBLIN

24

THE BARRACKS

Known for many years as the Royal Barracks, they were reputed to be among the largest in Europe and were designed by Colonel Thomas Burgh (architect also of Trinity College Library and of Dr Steevens' Hospital) and built in 1706. This applies only to the central square of the three visible in the plate, known in the eighteenth century as the Royal Square. To the left (West) of it is the Cavalry Square, and to the right (East) the Little Square, behind which is the Palatine Square. All these were added later in the eighteenth century, and early in the present century the original buildings by Burgh, in the centre, were removed, and the buildings are now known as Collins Barracks in memory of Michael Collins (1890–1922). The fields in the foreground of this plate have for long been part of Guinness's Brewery.

BARRACKS, DUBLIN.

VIEW OF DUBLIN FROM THE MAGAZINE FORT

This was the favourite point for general views of Dublin. The Magazine Fort from which the view is taken was ridiculed by Swift when it was built in about 1735: it is still there and still in military occupation. Sarah Bridge at Island-bridge, just half visible near the middle of the plate, was very new when the plate was taken, having been built in 1791, designed by Alexander Stevens. It is extremely graceful and still there though unfortunately little seen. The most conspicuous object on the skyline is the Royal Hospital, Kilmainham. In the distance just left of centre may be seen Dr. Steevens' Hospital, and on the extreme left the Military Infirmary. Other spires and domes such as St Patrick's Cathedral and the Four Courts can be made out.

VIEW of DUBLIN, from the MAGAZINE, PHOENIX-PARK.

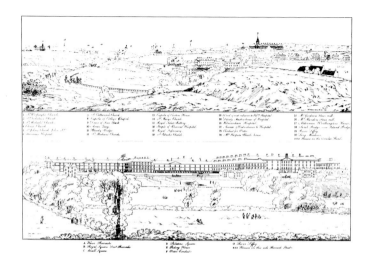

25a

KEY TO PLATES 24 AND 25

This key identifies the distant buildings visible on the Dublin skyline at the end of the eighteenth century and bears a remarkably unchanged likeness to the same view today.